•Contents•

KV-144-470

DEALING WITH FEELINGS

DEVELOPING VALUES

GOAL-SETTING

ATTITUDES

FUN STUFF

•About the Life Skills Series•

This series aims to provide the busy classroom teacher with practical ideas and strategies for developing and enhancing a set of valuable life skills in individual students.

There are numerous resources and articles about teaching values, dealing with grief, addressing bullying and the like, however, most of these articles and programs outline strategies for dealing with the problem at the whole-school level. While this is indeed a very appropriate way to deal with such matters, it has become obvious that there is a lack of ready-to-use materials for the actual classroom teacher. The Life Skills Series aims to fill the gap between the frameworks set out by national bodies and the delivery of practical and meaningful lessons in the classroom.

The Life Skills Series comprises four books:

Self-Esteem and Values

- Enhancing Self-Esteem of individuals
- Developing an awareness of feelings
- Promoting realistic goal-setting
- Enriching values in the classroom and community

Grief, Illness and Other Issues

- Coping with grief and loss
- Dealing with a disability or serious illness

Bullying and Conflict

- Coping with bullying at school
- Exploring conflict resolution through a problem solving approach

Family Relationships

- Discussing family roles
- Dealing with anger and other emotions
- Coping with separation, divorce and conflict

Each of the books in this series should be used as required. The series is not structured to be a complete program of work. Instead, it is designed as a valuable and practical resource for teachers that find themselves with students who are going through difficult life events.

Most of the activities are stand-alone – it is up to the teacher to decide what sheets will be relevant to the class. Some sheets will only be relevant to a select number of students, e.g. a bereaved student or a student who belongs to a blended family.

The themes in these four books overlap and so, when dealing with a particular issue, e.g. conflict resolution, activities from other books in this series might also be relevant to the situation that may exist in your classroom.

As well as student worksheets, all books contain extensive background notes for teachers, parents and students. Several sections contain annotated guides to relevant websites and literature resources available both online and in hard copy. Also included are extension ideas and teaching ideas for the classroom.

Internet References

Websites that are included in these four books can be accessed easily by visiting:

❑ **www.aber-publishing.co.uk**

Bookmark this page for ease of use.

Aber Education

Aber Education
Changing Lives

Life Skills Series

PHOTOCOPY MASTERS

Self

ues

dividuals
f feelings
cting
sroom

Blackburn
College

Library
01254 292120

Please return this book on or before the last date below

OUTCOME LINKED

By Jane Bourke

Life Skills Series

Self-Esteem and Values

(BLM)

© 2010 Aber Education and Jane Bourke

Printed in United Kingdom

ISBN: 978-1-84285-182-1

Author: Jane Bourke

Typesetting & Design: Shay Howard

Artwork: Terry Allen

BLACKBURN COLLEGE
LIBRARY

Acc. No. BB52735
Class No. UCL 373 ·011 4 BOU
Date 06-12-12

Published by:

Aber Publishing

PO Box 225

Abergele

www.aber-publishing.co.uk

info@aber-publishing.co.uk

COPYRIGHT NOTICE

Permission is granted for the purchaser to photocopy sufficient copies for non-commercial educational purposes. However, this permission is not transferable and applies only to the purchasing individual or institution.

Aber Education

•Extracts from Statutory Orders•

National Curriculum

Personal wellbeing key stage 3

Personal wellbeing: The personal development of pupils is a vital part of the key stage 3 curriculum. This non-statutory programme of study for personal wellbeing is intended to support schools in developing coherent whole-school approaches to personal, social, health and economic wellbeing (PSHE). It provides a context for schools to fulfil their legal responsibilities to promote the wellbeing of pupils and provide sex and relationships and drugs education. It also provides schools with an opportunity to focus on delivery of the skills identified in the framework for Social and Emotional Aspects of Learning (SEAL). The presentation and headings of this programme of study are the same as the programmes of study for other subjects to support cross-curricular planning. This programme of study replaces the non-statutory framework for personal, social and health education. The content is based on the EveryChild Matters outcomes and on the government's guidance on sex and relationships education.

Personal development: Personal wellbeing makes a significant contribution to young people's personal development and character. It creates a focus on the social and emotional aspects of effective learning, such as self-awareness, managing feelings, motivation, empathy and social skills. These five aspects of learning, identified within the SEAL framework, make an important contribution to personal wellbeing.

Evidence of this, drawn from personal wellbeing provision, can contribute to schools' self-evaluation forms.

Key concepts

There are a number of key concepts that underpin the study of personal wellbeing. Pupils need to understand these concepts in order to deepen and broaden their knowledge, skills and understanding.

Personal identities
a. Understanding that identity is affected by a range of factors, including a positive sense of self.
b. Recognising that the way in which personal qualities, attitudes, skills and achievements are evaluated affects confidence and self-esteem.
c. Understanding that self-esteem can change with personal circumstances, such as those associated with family and friendships, achievements and employment.

Healthy lifestyles
a. Recognising that healthy lifestyles, and the wellbeing of self and others, depend on information and making responsible choices.
b. Understanding that physical, mental, sexual and emotional health affect our ability to lead fulfilling lives, and that there is help and support available when they are threatened.
c. Dealing with growth and change as normal parts of growing up.

Personal identities: Understanding the factors that contribute to personal identities is essential if pupils are to accept and value themselves and develop confidence and self-esteem, maintain their mental/emotional health, make the most of their attributes and abilities, and celebrate achievements. Links can be made with citizenship and religious education when pupils address the key concepts of identities and diversity, which require understanding to be further developed in a local, national and global context.

Healthy lifestyles: A person's ability to stay healthy is affected by physical, mental, emotional, social, environmental and economic circumstances. Pupils should learn that they need to make informed decisions about behaviours and consider the short- and long-term consequences of their actions on themselves and others.

Personal wellbeing key stage 3

Risk
a. Understanding risk in both positive and negative terms and understanding that individuals need to manage risk to themselves and others in a range of situations.
b. Appreciating that pressure can be used positively or negatively to influence others in situations involving risk.
c. Developing the confidence to try new ideas and face challenges safely, individually and in groups.

Relationships
a. Understanding that relationships affect everything we do in our lives and that relationship skills have to be learnt and practised.
b. Understanding that people have multiple roles and responsibilities in society and that making positive relationships and contributing to groups,teams and communities is important.
c. Understanding that relationships can cause strong feelings and emotions.

Diversity
a. Appreciating that, in our communities, there are similarities as well as differences between people of different race, religion, culture, ability or disability, gender, age or sexual orientation.
b. Understanding that all forms of prejudice and discrimination must be challenged at every level in our lives.

Risk: Risk is an important part of everyday life. Having the confidence to take risks is essential to enjoying and achieving in learning and life. However, the ability to recognise, assess and manage risk is essential to physical safety and mental and emotional wellbeing. The concept of risk is also relevant to financial capability, enterprise and career choices, so links should be made to economic wellbeing and financial capability.

Relationships: The ability to develop relationships with a wide range of people is essential to being healthy, staying safe, enjoying and achieving, being able to make a positive contribution to society and achieving economic wellbeing.

Feelings and emotions: The National Healthy Schools Programme (emotional health and wellbeing theme) requires that 'the school has clear, planned opportunities for pupils to understand and explore feelings using appropriate learning and teaching styles'. The SEAL programme, which develops pupils' social skills and emotional resilience, can help schools cover the emotional health and wellbeing theme within the Healthy Schools Programme.

Aber Education

Diversity: This concept links with both personal identities and relationships. When pupils consider their attitude and behaviour towards diversity, they should identify similarities as well as differences between people. Learning to empathise with others helps pupils accommodate difference in their lives and accept their responsibility to challenge prejudice and discrimination wherever it is encountered. They learn to deal with challenges and accommodate diversity in all its forms

Critical reflection

Pupils should be able to:
a. reflect critically on their own and others' values
b. reflect on personal strengths, achievements and areas for development
c. recognise how others see them and give and receive feedback
d. identify and use strategies for setting and meeting personal targets in order to increase motivation
e. reflect on feelings and identify positive ways of understanding, managing and expressing strong emotions and challenging behaviour
f. develop self-awareness by reflecting critically on their behaviour and its impact on others.

Decision-making and managing risk

Pupils should be able to:
a. use knowledge and understanding to make informed choices about safety, health and wellbeing
b. find information and support from a variety of sources
c. assess and manage the element of risk in personal choices and situations
d. use strategies for resisting unhelpful peer influence and pressure
e. know when and how to get help
f. identify how managing feelings and emotions effectively supports decision-making and risk management.

Skills and processes: The SEAL skills have much in common with these key processes, and much of the language is similar. For example, the SEAL skills of self-awareness and managing feelings are important for critical reflection; motivation is an important dimension of decision-making; and empathy, social skills and managing feelings are required for developing relationships and working with others. Schools will wish to plan use of the SEAL materials and their teaching of the personal wellbeing programme of study so that pupils have a coherent learning experience.

Critical reflection: This involves asking probing questions such as 'How do I know that information is accurate?', 'What does it tell me about choices I should make?', 'How could I behave differently?' and 'What is the impact of my behaviour on others?'. Critical reflection can also help pupils develop self-awareness, enabling them to use their knowledge and experience of how they think and feel to choose their behaviour, plan their learning and build positive relationships.

Values: There are many complex and often conflicting values in society, and the exploration of these and clarification of personal values is an important part of personal wellbeing.

Strengths, achievements and areas for development: This links closely with learning for economic wellbeing and financial capability. Care should be taken to avoid repetition. This could include understanding motivation, viewing errors as part of the normal learning process and responding positively to disappointment or failure.

Positive ways of understanding: This includes pupils predicting what makes them angry or upset, and realising when feelings are 'taking over'.

Decision-making and managing risk: This involves finding and using accurate information, weighing up the options and identifying the risks and consequences of each option in order to make an informed choice. These skills can be applied to most situations, including those that involve issues relating to health, personal safety, relationships, personal and social change, leisure and learning opportunities. The ability to assess risk and consequences is particularly important when pupils are learning outside the classroom.

Developing relationships and working with others
Pupils should be able to:
a. use social skills to build and maintain a range of positive relationships
b. use the social skill of negotiation within relationships, recognising their rights and responsibilities and that their actions have consequences
c. use the social skills of communication, negotiation, assertiveness and collaboration
d. value differences between people and demonstrate empathy and a willingness to learn about people different from themselves
e. challenge prejudice and discrimination assertively.

Developing relationships and working with others: Social and emotional aspects of learning are important for personal and social development and for challenging inappropriate behaviour safely. This includes the ability to listen actively, empathise and understand the consequences of aggressive, passive and assertive behaviour in relationships.

Negotiation: This could include using a range of strategies to solve problems and resolve conflicts, for example using mediation to settle a dispute.

Relationships: This includes features of friendships and dealing with breakdown in friendships. In discussing positive relationships, the negative aspects of some relationships, including use of violence and other forms of abuse, may arise and should be addressed.

Impact of prejudice, bullying, discrimination and racism: Links should be made with the school's anti-bullying policy, including the importance of challenging homophobic bullying, compliance with the Race Relations

Amendment Act and the requirement for schools to promote community/ social cohesion.

Personal wellbeing helps young people embrace change, feel positive about who they are and enjoy healthy, safe, responsible and fulfilled lives

Aber Education

Teachers' Notes: Focusing on the Individual

The transition from primary to secondary schooling can prove to be one of the most daunting times of a student's life. Moving to the unknown territory of a high school from an environmentwhere the student is familiar, can incite feelings of self doubt and fear. Students are often surrounded by stories from older siblings and friends and may already have pre-conceived ideas of their own about secondary schooling. This book does not attempt to be an introduction to high school, but aims to promote and develop essential life skills that students can use to mak this transition a time of self-discovery and personal fulfilment.

The development of a healthy Self-Esteem and the instilling of traditional values complement each other in the quest to equip students with the life skills they need to succeed. If students are to foster personal values such as respect, responsibility and tolerance, then they need to have respect for themselves and this can only be achieved with a healthy Self-image.

In life, students need to be able to form close personal relationships, accept criticism, identify between positive and negative attitudes, take acceptable risks, exercise a degree of self control, take pride in their accomplishments, take responsibility for their actions and be able to communicate their feelings. The activities and resources in this book aim to provide opportunities for personal growth and reflection.

Self Awareness

This book endeavours to enhance a pastoral care program that may be running at your school. While it is not an entire program in itself, the activities merely act to provide meaningful and relevant learning opportunities for students who may be displaying signs of low Self-Esteem and Self-image. The tasks aim to equip students with the knowledge of how to go about clarifying goals, realising self worth and getting the most out of life, while at the same time practising a set of values and coping strategies that are reflected in societal and cultural traditions.

Self-Esteem

No discussion on life skills would be complete without a central focus on developing a healthy Self-Esteem. Students' Self-Esteem affects all aspects of their general performance teand well being. The activities allow students to explore their individuality. Many of the sheets should be private and students should not feel pressured to share personal information in what can sometimes be a threatening whole-class environment. Instead, encourage partner and small group work, allowing ample time for reflection and discussion.

Goal-Setting

Before any kind of realistic goals can be set, students should spend time getting to know themselves as individuals. They need to see that they, as individuals, are unique, and will possess different strengths and weaknesses to the person that they sit next to. An examination of the goal-setting process is given. Again, students should be encouraged to reflect on their choices and to understand that their long term goals may change over time.

Values

Values education is an important part of any school curriculum. The teaching of values is inherent in all subject areas but time should be taken to address each value in a way that students can reflect on the role of such a value in the wider community.

Evaluation and Assessment

Students' achievement in the areas covered in this book cannot be accurately measured on paper. Talk to individual students, record their behaviour as they complete the tasks and provide opportunities for self assessment by asking students to reflect on the activities with peers.

Ideally, have the students create a personal "Life Skills" folder for this unit. Allow them to keep all of their written materials in this folder. Encourage students to revisit their thoughts in a year or two, particularly as they approach the onset of secondary education – a time that can sometimes mean a major upheaval in the individual student's psyche, where many students experience difficulty in adjusting to the changing academic and social demands that secondary schooling can inflict.

Teachers' Notes: Enhancing Self-Esteem

Students who are experiencing difficulties at school, both academically and socially, often have a low Self-image and Self-Esteem.

Much has been written about how to raise self-esteem and this book adopts the approach that students really need to get to know themselves before they can start to develop meaningful and achievable goals in life.

Ideally, the activities should be used sequentially, however, they can be adapted and used as a stand alone resource as required. The activities are designed to make self-analysis fun.

The first section of this book explores feelings and how students can deal with strong emotions that they may experience. At the core of all activities is the belief that a range of feelings is normal and that it is the ways in which people deal with feelings that needs to be addressed. Opportunities are provided for students to analyse their own coping strategies and resilience.

The next learning focus heads towards an exploration of personal tastes, strengths and weaknesses. Most of the time, students know what they like and don't like and where their skills lie, however, by actually writing them down, students are able to have a closer examination and it provides a measure or base for students to reflect on further down the track.

Practical Ideas for Classroom Use

❑ Encourage teamwork without competitiveness – create opportunities where students can stand back and be proud of their results. Include opportunities for sharing and talking about feelings and situations they have experienced. Provide opportunities for students to mix with students out of their immediate circle by placing them in random groups of 3-4 students.

❑ Divide the class into groups of 6-8. Ask students to think about their classmates and what they like about each person. Students write ONE positive word to describe each person in their group, e.g. happy, helpful, caring, cheerful, funny. Ask students to write the actual person's name in small letters under the word so that they know who to give the word to later on, pointing out that students do not write their own name anywhere on the page. Students then cut out each word and make a pile of their words. In their groups they exchange "words" with others by fastening them to a students' back using either sticky tape or masking tape. When the "exchange" of words is over, students then sit in their groups and study words that they were given. The activity can be carried out as a whole class or groups can be mixed up so as to allow each student to write a word for all other students. The more words that a student receives, the more that certain character traits will be reflected, e.g. a student may end up with four or five words saying "caring" or "clever". This activity also provides opportunities for students to see how their peers view them.

❑ Set up a buddy system between your class and a junior class at the school. Each student is to be assigned a buddy that the student must plan activities for and act as a mentor.

Literary Resources

Lawrence, Denis (1996), _Enhancing Self-esteem in the Classroom_, 2nd Ed. Sage Publications Inc. California, USA. ISBN: 1853963518.

Mosley, J. & Sonnet, H. (2002) _101 Games for Self-Esteem_, ISBN: 1855033518

Mosley, J. & Murray, P. (1996) _Quality Circle Time in the Primary Classroom: Your Essential Guide to Enhancing Self-esteem, Self-discipline & Positive Relationships_, LDA Publishers, New York, USA. ISBN: 1855032295

Online Resources
❑ **www.self-esteem-nase.org/links.shtml - Self-Esteem Links**
❑ **www.circle-time.co.uk/store.html - Jenny Mosley Consultancies**

Aber Education

Websites for Teachers

❑ **www.livingvalues.net/** - Values Education for Children and Young Adults
This site was developed as an innovative values education problem solver and offers a wide variety of experiential values activities and practical techniques to educators, facilitators, parents and caregivers that enable children and young adults to explore and develop twelve universal values. In addition to programs for classrooms and parent groups, the site also has special materials for street children, children affected by war, and children affected by earthquakes.

❑ **www.curriculum.edu.au/values/** - Values Education
A teacher resource and professional development site to support values education in Australian schools.

❑ **www.andrewfuller.com.au/research/valueBoysGirls.pdf** - Valuing Boys, Valuing Girls
Contains notes for a presentation by clinical psychologist Andrew Fuller, at the Centre for Excellence in Teaching Conference (2002).

❑ **www.self-esteem-nase.org/** - National Association for Self-Esteem
This American site contains some relevant resources and articles related to promoting a healthy Self-Esteem. Check ▶ **www.self-esteem-nase.org/whatisselfesteem.shtml** for definitions.

❑ **www.acer.edu.au/tests/school/avq/intro.html** - Attitudes and Values Questionnaire (ACER)
Contains questionnaires that can be downloaded from this site and used in the classroom to gauge students social and emotional growth as well as their conscience and compassion. Can be used as a whole school assessment rather than for individual assessment.

❑ **www.womhealth.org.au/studentfactsheets/bodyimage.htm** - Body Image and Self-Esteem
Student fact sheets aimed at adolescents, however, upper primary children may benefit.

❑ **www.kidsource.com/kidsource/content2/Strengthen_Children_Self.html** - Strengthening Children's Self-Esteem Contains relevant articles and references.

❑ **www.cln.org/themes/self_esteem.html** - Self-Esteem Theme Page
Contains an excellent list of pertinent links for this area of development. Some of the links are appropriate for children, however, most are directed towards the teacher.

❑ **www.eduref.org/cgi-bin/res.cgi/Subjects/Health/Mental_Emotional_Health**
Lesson plans for developing Self-Esteem.

❑ **www.cyberparent.com/esteem/** - About Self-Esteem in Children
An excellent site for parents.

❑ **www.youthealth.com/** - YouthHealth
This commercial site develops fun and responsible resources for the classroom. Activities allow students to take a journey of exploration and discovery into health and the human body using the site's health education software resources. Contains child-centred health education resources for students and teachers, combining curriculum-based content (UK) with dynamic information, activities and games.

❑ **www.kiwican.telecom.co.nz** - Kiwi Can
This New Zealand youth programme is the first and only full-time, privately operated needs-based life skills and values-based programme implemented in primary and intermediate schools in New Zealand. It aims to challenge and develop the students in a positive way to increase their physical fitness, mental awareness, creative abilities and understanding and implementation of values and life skills.

•DEALING WITH FEELINGS•

❏ **kidshealth.org/kid/feeling/emotion/self_esteem. html** - Learning about Self-Esteem

❏ **www.kidshealth.org/kid/feeling/** - Dealing with Feelings Contains sections on:
- School issues - bullying, cheating, repeating a year level;
- Home issues - living with grandparents, homesickness, moving, running away, being a twin, trouble with siblings;
- Friend issues - peer pressure, gossip, kids with special needs;
- Emotional issues - Self-Esteem, phobias, grief, anger, disorders, mental illness.

❏ **www.shykids.com/** - Shy Kids is a site developed by former "shy kids" and aims to offer practical advice to children, teens and their parents on how to build confidence and make friends.

❏ **www.youthealth.com/** - Youth Health
Allows students to take a virtual journey of exploration and discovery into health and the human body using the site's health education software resources. Contains child-centred health education resources for students and teachers, combining curriculum-based content with dynamic information, activities and games.

❏ **www.planetpals.com/index.html** - Planet Pals aims to link up kids around the planet.

❏ **www.buffalolib.org/kidscorner/greatbooks/books_ selfesteem.asp** - This site contains an extensive list of appropriate books that explore Self-Esteem.

❏ **pbskids.org/itsmylife/** - It's My Life. Explores emotions and examines depression and feelings of fear and anger. The site also contains informative sections about the body, school, family and friends.

see http://www.helpself.com/directory/esteem.htm

Activity 1 — In Touch With Your Feelings

Feeling Unhappy?

Have you ever felt like not wanting to leave the house? Have you ever felt like yelling at someone? Have you ever been so angry that you felt like your head was going to explode?

Feeling Happy?

Have you ever been so happy that you felt like telling the whole world?

Maybe you DID tell the whole world? Maybe you hugged someone you didn't even know! Maybe you forgot about every other thing in the whole world – just for a minute!

Feeling Sad?

Ever felt so sad about something that it was all you could think about?

Maybe you wanted to cry, maybe you wanted to talk to someone, maybe you just wanted to be alone

Feeling Scared

Ever felt so scared that you got a funny feeling in your stomach? Maybe you started shivering, maybe you felt tense, maybe you thought your heart was going to jump right out of your chest?

Does any of this sound familiar to you?

Well guess what? This means you're normal!

From time to time EVERYONE feels strong emotions and this is OK. What is important is the way in which you DEAL with your emotions.

You may have been HAPPY because you won something, or maybe you got a new baby brother or sister! Maybe you scored the highest marks in a test or maybe you got to go on an overseas holiday!

How did you show or express your feelings?

❑ _____

❑ _____

❑ _____

You may have been UNHAPPY when someone let you down, perhaps you were hurt in an accident or maybe someone just annoyed you, for no reason!

How did you show or express your feelings?

❑ _____

❑ _____

❑ _____

You may have been SAD when you lost something. Maybe someone close to you died, or maybe you just thought that there was nothing to be happy about

How did you show or express your feelings?

❑ _____

❑ _____

❑ _____

You may have been SCARED when you were left alone, or when other kids were bullying you or when the family car ran out of petrol in the middle of nowhere ... in the dark!

How did you show or express your feelings?

❑ _____

❑ _____

❑ _____

HOW DO YOU FEEL MOST OF THE TIME?

_____

_____

_____

_____

_____

Activity 2 — What is Happiness?

❑ Does the smell of roses make you happy? ❑ Does eating spaghetti make you happy?

❑ Does waiting in line at the supermarket make you happy?

❑ Does having to clean out the birdcage make you happy?

What makes you happy?

Write down five things that make you happy.

Happiness Rating ☺

❑ _____ ▸ _____

❑ _____ ▸ _____

❑ _____ ▸ _____

❑ _____ ▸ _____

❑ _____ ▸ _____

Write down five things that make you unhappy.

❑ _____ ▸ _____

❑ _____ ▸ _____

❑ _____ ▸ _____

❑ _____ ▸ _____

❑ _____ ▸ _____

Rate each of your statements above
according to the scale below.
Write the number in the boxes above.

1   2   3   4   5   6   7   8   9   10.

VERY unhappy   Fairly unhappy   A little bit unhappy

Yippee!

chucka–sput! sput! sput! click!

E.g. People fighting might make you feel unhappier than when someone steals the last cookie out of the jar. So for people fighting you might put 1 and for when someone steals the last cookie you might put 9.

Aber Education

Activity 3	When I Am Not Happy ...

Think of a time when you have not been happy and complete the UNHAPPY log below.

Date of unhappiness:

_____

Estimated time of unhappiness:

_____

Reasons for feeling unhappy?

_____

How did you deal with this?
List four things that you did.

❑ _____

❑ _____

❑ _____

❑ _____

What remedies might have made you feel better at the time?

_____

_____

Five words that described how you felt:

❑ _____

❑ _____

❑ _____

❑ _____

❑ _____

Recommendations for future happiness:

_____

_____

_____

Hmm, what symptoms do you have?

Activity 4	Survival Sheet

There are times when we don't feel happy.

Instead, we may feel sad, angry, jealous or scared.

In the boxes below, list two times when you have felt like the guy in the picture. They may be times that happened a long time ago, or they may be times that happened last week!

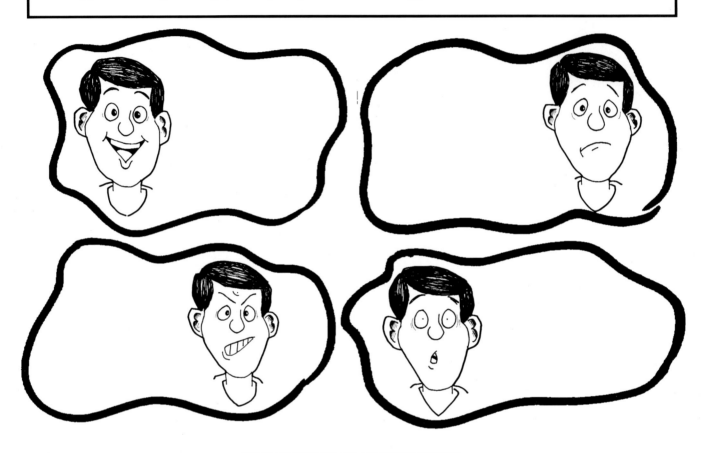

Survival Plan

What are some things you can do when you are not feeling happy?

Write your own personal plan for dealing with things when you are not happy.

- _____
- _____
- _____
- _____
- _____
- _____
- _____
- _____

Aber Education

Activity 5 — Learning About Me

In order for me to be happy, I need to know all about me. I need to know what things will make me feel happy and what things will make me feel proud of myself. If I know myself then I can begin to set goals and think about what I want to achieve in life. If I don't know myself then I may find I am just running around in circles with no direction in life at all!

What do you think about ?

Find the best word for each statement below.
You may like to choose more than one. Circle the best word:

School is ...	fun	boring	easy	hard	exciting	scary	cool
Weekends are ...	great	boring	happy	sad	lonely	short	interesting
Sport is ..	fun	easy	hard	boring	scary	scary	embarrassing
Maths is ...	hard	dull	stupid	fun	easy	annoying	daggy
Cockroaches are ...	pretty	beautiful	creepy	ugly	dirty	tasty	interesting
My friends are ...	caring	messy	funny	sad	silly	happy	clever
My pet is ...	messy	stupid	cute	loving	scary	friendly	happy
My family is ...	friendly	crazy	loud	grumpy	daggy	happy	quiet

My favourite subject at school is: _____

My favourite sport that I like to participate in is: _____

My favourite sport that I like to watch is: _____

My favourite hobbies are: _____

My favourite book is: _____

My favourite movie is: _____

My favourite music is: _____

My favourite singers are: _____

My favourite place to relax is: _____

My favourite thing to do when I relax is: _____

My favourite friends are: _____

_____

On my birthday I like to: _____

_____

If I could wish for anything, it would be: _____

_____

My ideal holiday would be: _____

_____

Morning Fred, Long time no see! What have you been up to?

Hi Fred!

Activity 6 — Things I Can Do

Most people feel good about themselves when they think of all the things that they have achieved. Personal satisfaction makes them feel pleased with themselves.

Look at your life so far. Ever since you were born, you made steps towards goals:

- ❏ Think about learning to crawl.
- ❏ Think about when you first started to read.
- ❏ Think about when you first learnt to ride a bike without stabilizers/trainer wheels.
- ❏ Think about when you hit that first tennis ball over the net.
- ❏ Think about when you scored that first goal in your favourite sport.
- ❏ Think about the first time you dived off the high diving board.

These are all personal achievements and are things that made your parents proud.

Make a list of your major achievements in life so far. Draw some pictures to illustrate and paste a picture of yourself under the heading in the box.

Picture of me

My Achievements So Far!

❏ At Home	❏ At School
❏ In the Community	❏ With My Friends
❏ In Sport	❏ In Other Areas

Aber Education

Activity 7   An Interview With Yourself

Have a careful read of the sentence beginnings below. Think about how you would finish the sentence. There are no right or wrong answers. Be very honest – only write what you feel otherwise you could be telling lies to yourself! You can keep this sheet private or you may like to share with a friend.

1. I like people who _____

2. I don't like people who _____

3. I feel happy about myself when _____

4. I am angry with myself when _____

5. My sister/brother annoys me when _____

6. My friend makes me happy when _____

7. My friend annoys me when _____

8. At school, I do my best when I feel _____

9. On the playing field, I do my best when I feel _____

10. My strengths are _____

11. My weaknesses are _____

12. When I like something I have done I _____

13. When I don't like something I have done I _____

14. When I see people fighting I _____

15. When I see people who are sad I _____

16. When I see people who are happy I _____

17. If I could do ANYTHING at all I wanted today it would be _____

18. The best thing that could happen to me EVER is _____

19. Two things I want to become better at are _____

20. Spend some time on this one ...

    In the future, I want _____

    _____

    _____

Teachers' Notes: Values

In recent years much emphasis has been placed on the teaching of values in the classroom. Remember, the most important way to teach values is by example.

Immerse the students in a values-rich environment by:

❑ promoting respect, honesty and trust among all students;
❑ encouraging a cohesive and friendly class climate;
❑ providing opportunities to learn about high achievers;
❑ instilling a healthy set of ideals and values through practical and relevant activities, in the classroom, whole-school environment and wider community.

Teaching Approaches

Values should not be taught in isolation. Core values are inherent in all subject areas and values can be taught through different learning styles, particularly with group learning and collaboration. Students should be given ample opportunities to reflect on their work at all times, particularly with the activities in this book which should act as a springboard for further personal development.

While values education should be adopted as a whole school approach, it is important that teachers promote healthy sets of values among students and to understand that values will be acquired and instilled at different levels among individual students.

Values to promote in the classroom and school environment include:

❑ Tolerance and Understanding
❑ Respect
❑ Social Justice
❑ Excellence
❑ Care
❑ Inclusion and Trust
❑ Honesty
❑ Freedom
❑ Being Ethical

Other Individual Values:

❑ Compassion
❑ Responsibility

❑ Self-discipline
❑ Healthy Self-image
❑ Perseverance
❑ Courage
❑ Cooperation
❑ Resilience

Instilling such values will allow a student to:

❑ Decide his/her own future
❑ Have control of his/her life
❑ Earn respect from others
❑ Form close relationships

❑ Develop self-respect
❑ Own and care for things

❑ Respect privacy

❑ Demonstrate self control

❑ Exercise will power

❑ Keep safe

❑ Develop a sense of belonging
❑ Strive for self-improvement
❑ Have fun

❑ Take risks

❑ Be all he/she can be
❑ Acquire wisdom
❑ Build character
❑ Respect all living things
❑ Maintain good health
❑ Understand his/herself
❑ Reach for success and achievement
❑ Enjoy a challenging life
❑ Seek variety and excitement
❑ Have the freedom to choose
❑ Find meaning and purpose in life
❑ Have a concern for others
❑ Be a law abiding citizen
❑ Develop close family relationships

Useful Websites

▸ **www.teachingvalues.com/**
- Teaching Values. An excellent resource for teachers, parents and students.

▸ **http://cornerstonevalues.org/ we really like this and couldn't find a UK version**

▸ **Association for Living Values Education** International worldwide community of values educators. Based in Switzerland, see http://www.livingvalues.net/support.html#Europe for European connections, http://www.livingvalues.net/support.html#North%20America for USA/Canada

Practical Ideas for Values Education

All About Me

Students complete an Individual Learning Project (ILP) about themselves. Sections could include: photos, drawings, stories, poems, history, family tree diagrams, friendship circles, hobbies and interests, special people, personal goals, achievements so far, people they admire, favourites. Each project should include a special page about how each student sees him or herself in ten years time.

Group Challenges

Assign a special time each week that can be devoted to group challenges. Every week the group members should change so that students are given opportunities to work with all class members and not just students in their immediate circle or seating arrangement. The easiest way to do this is to randomly number students 1-5 each week and then ask all the number 1s, 2s and so on to group together. To make things even more child-focused, ask students to determine the challenges that groups must accomplish.

Challenges can include tasks such as:

❑ "Devise ten ways to save water in our school environment."

❑ "Plan a practical community outing to demonstrate respect."

❑ "Make a poster to show ways to use recycled materials in the classroom."

Note: Students to brainstorm and suggest challenges as an individual written task prior to the setting up of the group challenges.

Community Visits

❑ ***Day Care / Pre-Primary Centre***: In pairs, students to write stories with themes such as caring for the environment, honesty, responsibility, self-discipline and perseverance. These stories can then be "published" on the computer and students can colourfully illustrate their work. Students then read these stories to the pre-primary children.

❑ ***Senior Citizens, Retirement Village:*** Students to perform brief skits and songs for the elderly.

❑ Encourage students to participate in community fundraising events.

❑ Encourage participation in community litter collection and recycling activities.

Internet Activities

❑ Establish e-mail communication with school students in other countries. This site has a list of excellent links: ▸ **www.theteacherspot.com/ student_penpals.html** Teacher Spot

❑ In groups, students to create personal web pages for their class (leave out student surnames!) that demonstrate ways in which the class contributes to the school and community.

❑ Students to familiarise themselves with local community websites – paying attention to upcoming events and activities.

❑ Students to research topics such as:

Recycling ▸ **www.cansmart.org/** - CanSmart ▸ **www.ollierecycles.com.au/** - Ollie's World ▸ **www.planetark.org** - Planet Ark ▸ **www. recyclingnearyou.com.au/** - Recycling Near You!

Saving Water - ▸ **www.myinternet.com.au/edu/ water_year/index.htm** - Don't Be a Drip, Save a Drop

Caring for the Environment - ▸ **www.kids-for-the-environment.com.au/**

Learning About Other Cultures - ▸ **www.ipl.org/ div/kidspace/cquest/** - Culture Quest World Tour

Other Cool Sites for Kids:

▸ **www.dosomething.org/** - Do Something!

▸ **www.nrdc.org/greensquad/** - Green Squad

▸ **www.greenscreen.org/** - Green Screen: Turning Kids Green

▸ **readyed.com.au/urls/enviro/** - Links for Our Environment

Developing Values: Student Activities (1)

☞ *Some of the ideas below can be demonstrated at school while others are ideas for community service.*

Respect:

- ❑ Entertain senior citizens at a retirement home – Class activity (i.e. read stories, choir singing).
- ❑ Correspond with students from another country and learn about each other's culture – Use the Internet.
- ❑ Write thank you letters to community leaders for their improvements to your local community.
- ❑ Volunteer to help the disabled at your school or in the community.
- ❑ Participate in fundraising activities for charities and other organisations.
- ❑ Volunteer to help with cleanup or gardening chores at a park or other public recreational area.
- ❑ Look for ways to help in any situation without being asked.
- ❑ Be friendly to someone who needs a friend.
- ❑ Think of ways you can help before people have to ask you!
- ❑ Sponsor a canned food drive at your school.
- ❑ Forgive someone who has hurt you.

Compassion:

- ❑ Research how other countries have cared for their citizens through history in times of greatest need such as through disasters, wars, poverty and famine.
- ❑ Make a "Welcome!" kit for a new student.
- ❑ Visit some sick children at a hospital. Take some stories in to read.
- ❑ Do a random act of kindness for someone who is sad.
- ❑ Offer to help an elderly neighbour by doing their gardening or running errands.
- ❑ Write in your journal about a time when someone was kind to you or did a service for you. How did you feel?
- ❑ A philanthropist is someone who has dedicated his or her life to improving the lives of others. Some well-known philanthropists include Burns Unit Specialist Dr Fiona Wood, Microsoft pioneer Bill Gates, rock stars such as Sting, Bono and Sir Bob Geldof and sporting legends such as Pat Rafter and Ian Thorpe. Check out some other famous philanthropists at

▸ **www.fdncenter.org/yip/youth_celebrity.html** on the Internet.

Perseverance:

- ❑ Try not to lose your temper! Write a list of ways to "chill out" and have a copy handy in your desk at school and in your room at home.
- ❑ When something doesn't work for you, try again and again.
- ❑ Try to finish what you start.
- ❑ Keep working at something that is difficult until you complete it.
- ❑ Don't give up on difficult jobs or situations. Think how good you will feel once you have finished.
- ❑ Reward yourself when you complete a difficult task.
- ❑ Brainstorm a list of ways for developing good study habits. Make a bright chart for the classroom. You may wish to do this activity with a friend or small group.

Cooperation:

- ❑ Be ready to lend a helping hand. Offer to help before having to be asked.
- ❑ When working or playing in groups, be the one to help the group reach an agreement.
- ❑ Help find a compromise when a group is in disagreement.
- ❑ Learn to be a good loser. Remember it is only a game. Your turn as winner will come!
- ❑ Invite someone who is alone or "left out" to join your activity.
- ❑ Make a poster for your local shopping centre that promotes cooperation in the community.
- ❑ Brainstorm community service ideas.
- ❑ Contribute clothing to a community service organisation serving families in unfortunate circumstances.

Developing Values: Student Activities (2)

Self Discipline:

❑ In groups, brainstorm a list of problems that might result from a lack of self discipline. Make headings for personal appearance, physical/mental/emotional health, school success, life success, friendships, job performance, talents, participation in community clubs and so on.

❑ Do silly exercises to strengthen your self discipline like not scratching, or not biting your nails.

❑ In pairs, perform role-plays to demonstrate how you might talk with a younger brother or sister who is showing a lack of self discipline.

❑ Write a creative story about a make-believe character (e.g. hero, villain) who has no self discipline.

❑ Internet research: Look up scientists, engineers, doctors, and other people to learn the role of self discipline in training for their careers and in working. This site is an excellent starting point: ▸ **www.achievement.org/ autodoc/pagegen/galleryachieve.html** - Academy of Achievement

Honesty:

❑ Thank someone in your family for being honest.

❑ Tell someone (e.g. your parents, teacher or best friend) about a mistake you've made that you've been keeping a secret.

❑ Compliment a friend for being honest.

❑ Tell a funny story without exaggerating.

❑ Express your real feelings without anger, without blaming others, without exaggerating, and without hurting the feelings of someone else.

❑ If you find something, hand it into lost property. Think how you would feel if something you lost was returned to you.

❑ If you ask someone for their honest opinion, stay calm if their opinion isn't what you wanted to hear.

❑ Write a story with an honesty theme for pre-primary students. Illustrate your work and turn it into a book. Read your story to students or your younger brothers and sisters.

🖱 Check out these Websites:

❑ **library.thinkquest.org/J001709/**
- Values – Making Choices For Life

❑ **www.sptimes.com/nie/nieanne.html**
- Anne Frank: Lessons in Human Rights and Dignity

❑ **www.tolerance.org/pt/**
- Planet Tolerance

❑ **www.immi.gov.au/multicultural/harmony/**
- Living in Harmony

❑ **http://www.soton.ac.uk/mediacentre/news/2006/ mar/06_30.shtml**Achieving extraordinary things against the odds - Portraits put women high achievers in the limelight

❑ **www.belonging.org/**
- A Century Celebrated

❑ **www.webquestdirect.com.au/championsofjustice/**
- Webquest: Champions of Justice

❑ **http://www.nelsonmandela.org/index.php** read the remarkable true story of a great man

Activity 8	Groups and Belonging

☞ *This activity will work better if you work in small groups. At the end, choose a person in your group to report to the rest of the class.*

Cultural and Social Groups

Think of some of the groups to which you belong. For example, sporting groups, religious groups, interest groups, family groups, charity groups, disability groups, ethnic groups and so on. Think about the groups that you have no choice over. Complete the table below by writing the various groups in to which you belong. Divide the groups so that you have a list of the groups that you had a choice about joining, e.g. *your local swimming club team*, and the groups in which you do NOT have a choice with, e.g. *your family group.*

Groups I Belong To	Groups Where I Have No Choice
e.g. Gymnastics class	Member of Italian community
	Year 7 class at school

Sharing Information

Share your table with other students in your small group.

Found out some of the groups that other students belong to. Write down these groups using the headings below.

• **Other groups that students belong to within my class:** *e.g. choir*

• **Groups that exist within my school:** *e.g. netball team*

• **Groups that exist within my community:** *e.g. Chinese community, Indian community, Jewish community, volunteer fire brigade*

Group Discussion

Discuss the following points in your group.

❑ Look at each student's group table and discuss the differences among each table.

❑ How are the members of each group different? Talk about one of YOUR groups.

❑ How are all the groups the same? Does each group have rules?

❑ What are some groups you belong to where you do not have a choice? How do you feel about this group?

❑ What are some groups that you cannot belong to? Why?

❑ What groups do you enjoy being a member of? Why?

❑ What makes each group special?

❑ Why do people form groups?

Aber Education

Activity 9	Someone to Look Up To

☞ *Read about some of the great achievers in our world. You may like to focus on someone from history or you may want to study someone who exists in today's world. You may even like to choose from the list of achievers below.*

- Nelson Mandela
- Stephen Hawking
- Neil Armstrong
- Sir Edmund Hillary
- Nicole Kidman

- Cathy Freeman
- Alexander Graham Bell
- Helen Keller
- Delta Goodrem
- Captain James Cook

- Sir Donald Bradman
- Albert Einstein
- Ludwig van Beethoven
- Ian Thorpe
- Bill Gates

Check out these websites

The Role Model Project http://www.achieversuk.com/

Yorkshire Young chievers http://www.yorkshireyoungachievers.co.uk/

Biographies: ▸ **www.ajkids.com** (Type in Biography and see where it takes you!)

Extra: ▸ **www.homeworkhotline.com/Biographies.htm**

Complete the report below

Name of person: _____

Date of birth: _____

Nationality: _____

Brief background: _____

_____

_____

Major life achievements: _____

_____

_____

Significant points: (e.g. difficulties they have had to overcome, problems in their career, motivations for their goals)

_____

_____

_____

I respect this person because:

_____

_____

_____

Teachers' Notes: Goal-Setting

Many students' problems stem from a lack of perspective on what it is they hope to achieve. In many cases, students will think that talking about their goals is a waste of time. Goal-setting is not effective if the goals are not realistic or relevant to the person setting the goals. If a student agrees to a goal, purely because they think that is what his/her parents or teachers think they should be doing, then the student will most likely experience difficulty in achieving that goal.

Ideas for encouraging clear and meaningful goal-setting:

If you suddenly woke up and everything was perfect, what would your life be like?

On a scale of 1-10, how would you rate:

❑   Your life at home   ▸ _____

❑   Your time at school   ▸ _____

❑   Your friends   ▸ _____

❑   Your weekend activities   ▸ _____

❑   Your teachers   ▸ _____

How could you improve the ratings for each of the above?

❑   Your life at home _____
    _____

❑   Your time at school _____
    _____

❑   Your friends _____
    _____

❑   Your weekend activities _____
    _____

❑   Your teachers _____
    _____

Setting goals that address a particular issue:

What is the issue?

❑   On a scale of 1-10, how much are you prepared to improve this situation?
    _____

❑   On a scale of 1-10, how likely do you think this problem can be worked out?
    _____

❑   What would it mean to you to have this problem resolved?
    _____

❑   What smaller goals do you need to achieve before attempting to fix this situation?
    _____

Relevant Websites:

❑   **www.inspiringteachers.com/tips/goals/**
    - Tips for Teaching Kids Goal-Setting

❑   **www.ndt-ed.org/TeachingResources/ ClassroomTips/Goal_Setting.htm**
    - Teaching Goal-Setting

❑   **www.mygoals.com/**
    - This innovative site is aimed at allowing individuals to set and manage their own goals. They can be short term or long term goals and the site actually sends e-mail reminders to highlight what task students should be working on to arrive at their goals.

❑   **www.goalsguy.com/**
    - Goal-setting, personal development and motivation.

Aber Education

Activity 10 — What Am I Good At?

☞ *Not everyone is a legend on the playing field or a superstar on the stage or a genius at school. Some people are good at listening, some people are good at talking and some people are good at writing. Some people are good at tennis, some people are good at archery, and some people are very good at getting chocolate stains out of the carpet! Some people are good at noticing things, some people are good at hiding things and some people are good at making a lot of noise.*

Everyone is good at something. Some people are good at many different things, while others are very good at just one thing in particular. You will find that nearly everyone would like to be better at something.

Look at the students below:

Questin is good at asking questions ...

What is the meaning of life?

Chatta is good at telling jokes ...

Ok, a funny thing happened on the way to the canteen ...

Spella is good with words ...

I love homophones and adverbs.

Make a list of the things that you think YOU are good at.

Include in your list things that other people might think you are good at.

The things you list will be known as your strengths.

 MY STRENGTHS

- _____
- _____
- _____
- _____
- _____
- _____
- _____
- _____
- _____
- _____
- _____
- _____
- _____
- _____

Activity 11 — What Am I Not So Good At?

👉 *No one is perfect. Everybody has something that they are not so good at. This is OK. This is what makes us normal people.*

I draw like Mr Squiggle.

I can't do aerobics. I am very uncoordinated.

I can't run fast.

Questin is not good at telling jokes ...

Did you hear the joke about the question?

Chatta is not good with words ...

I knead to no moor abowt werds and speling.

Spella is not good at asking questions ...

What exactly is a question?

Make a list of the things that you think you are not so good at.

The things you list will be known as your weaknesses.

👎 MY WEAKNESSES

- _____
- _____
- _____
- _____
- _____
- _____
- _____
- _____
- _____
- _____
- _____
- _____
- _____
- _____

Aber Education

Activity 12 — Aiming For The Stars

 Have a good look at the lists you made showing your STRENGTHS and WEAKNESSES. You can use these lists to help you make some plans about what you might want to achieve in the future.

Look at the three students below. They have each recognised their strengths and thought about how they could use these strengths to achieve bigger things. They probably studied their weaknesses and thought about things that might stop them from achieving their goals.

If you know that you are afraid of flying, you are unlikely to set a long-term goal of wanting to become a flight attendant or a pilot. If you are shy, you are unlikely to want to become a party organiser!

Reflect back to your list of strengths.

What sorts of things do you think you may be able to achieve? For each strength that you listed, write down something that you may be able to achieve by developing that strength.

I would like to be an interviewer!

Questin (Remember – he is good at asking questions!)

I would like to be a stand up comedian!

Chatta (Remember – she is good at telling jokes!)

I would like to be a book editor!

Spella (Remember – she is good with words)

For example:

- **I am good at writing stories**

  I would like to create a book for the library.

- **I am good at gymnastics**

  I would like to try out for the state championships.

Activity 13 — My Life

👉 *Complete the boxes below. Keep this sheet for your own personal record. Put it in a safe place at home and remember — you do not have to show anyone. Check the sheet in a few months time or even a few years time. Reflect on how your attitudes have changed.*

Things I like about my life	Things I would like to change

Things I can change now	Things I would like to achieve in the future
	Today's Date: _____

Aber Education

Activity 14	This is Your Life (1)

☞ ❏ *Do you know what you want to achieve in life?* ❏ *Do you want to be really good at something?* ❏ *Do you want to be able to do a particular thing?* ❏ *Do you want to make a lot of money?* ❏ *Do you want to travel and see the world?* ❏ *Do you want to help other people who aren't as lucky as you? The answers to these questions are all things that will affect the types of choices you might make in life. You can change the things you want, you just have to remember to have a clear idea about what it is that you want. If you don't know what you want, how can you hope to get it?*

Look at the kids below. They all have different goals.

Sam: I want to be a chef.

Lilly: I want to learn how to play the guitar.

Todd: I want to swim the English Channel.

It is important to make goals for the short-term and goals for the long-term. Short-term goals include things we might be able to achieve this week or this month that will lead to achieving a long-term goal. Long-term goals are things we will take much longer to achieve. You might achieve these goals in a year or by the time you grow up to be an adult.

The kids above have told you their long-term goals. Their short-term goals might be ...

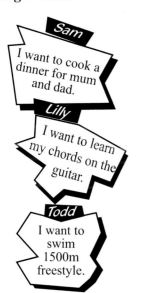

Sam: I want to cook a dinner for mum and dad.

Lilly: I want to learn my chords on the guitar.

Todd: I want to swim 1500m freestyle.

Look at the Goals below:

❶ **Underline the *short-term* goals in GREEN.**
  ❏ **Underline the *long-term* goals in RED.**
  ❏ **Then, match up the short-term goal with a long-term goal.**

I want to be a motor cross champion.

I want to be a mechanic

I want to start tennis lessons.

I want to get 100% in the maths test.

I want to play keyboards in a band.

I want to win the junior tennis championship.

I want to star in the school concert.

I want to save money for a bicycle.

I want to run a marathon.

I want to be a school gardener.

I want to be a mathematician.

I want to climb the rock wall at the recreation centre.

I want to plant some vegetable seeds.

I want to run around the oval five times.

I want to find out how an engine works.

I want to start piano lessons.

I want to climb Mount Everest.

I want to be an actor on Home and Away.

I want to do a first aid course.

I want to be a doctor.

Activity 15	This is Your Life (2)

We've all watched cartoons. You may have even seen the Roadrunner cartoons.
Think about that rascal Wile E. Coyote. He appears to have only ONE goal in life ... and that is to catch the Roadrunner.

Have you noticed that this crazy coyote never seems to achieve his goal? Maybe he needs to set more than one goal. Maybe he should think about setting goals that he knows he can achieve. These are called *realistic* or *achievable* goals.

You can have goals in a number of areas. Write down some goals for each box below. Think of all the things you might want to do or be or see!

Immediate Goal	Short-term Goal	Long-term Goal
AT HOME		
Today	By the end of the year	By the time I move out
WITH MY SCHOOL WORK		
Today	By the end of the year	By the time I leave school
IN SPORT		
Today	By the end of the year	By the time I leave school
MY RELATIONSHIPS WITH OTHERS		
Today	By the end of the year	By the time I leave school

Reflection Time

Did you find it hard to write some of your goals? Which ones? Keep this sheet in a very special place. You may want to look at it later. Your ideas about the goals you want to achieve may change depending on the time and the stage of life you are in. You will probably find that as you grow older you get a better idea as to what you hope to achieve in your life.

Aber Education

Activity 16 — Goals for Me

☞ *Do you ever feel like you are being told what you should do or what things you should try? Do you sometimes feel that you should be doing something in order to make someone else happy?*

Look at Martha below. Martha's mum was a model. She wanted Martha to be a model too. However, Martha doesn't really like trying on all the clothes or walking around in front of everyone and she isn't at all interested in fashion.

Martha really likes swimming. She wants to swim everyday and she would like to try out for the swimming team. Martha's mum says that she can't possibly do swimming, as it will ruin her hair for modelling classes.

What will Martha's mum think if Martha is no good at modelling?

How will Martha feel if she is not able to develop her swimming?

Write down what Martha might say to her mum about her feelings.

_____

_____

_____

_____

_____

_____

_____

_____

_____

_____

_____

_____

_____

_____

How could this situation be resolved so that everyone is happy?

Fill in the speech bubbles.

My Goals are for Me!

Has anyone ever told you that your goals are stupid? How did you feel?

What might you say to people who don't think you can achieve your goals?

Climbing to Success (1) Background Notes

☞ *Ever wanted to parachute out of a plane or maybe climb Mt Everest?*

It's certainly not an easy task! Careful planning needs to occur.

If you wanted to make climbing Mt Everest one of your goals in life, you wouldn't just wait until you were old enough and then book a flight to Nepal.

You would need to spend a LOT of time preparing. You might set some smaller short-term goals to make sure you're on the right track. You may find after trying to achieve some of these short-term goals that climbing isn't for you at all!

Pretend this is a picture of Mt Everest. There is a space for you at the top but before you get anywhere near the top, you have to reach the other levels.

Each level has a task that you would need to achieve that will keep you on the path to your goal.

6 **Climb to the top of Mount Everest!**

5 Climb a small mountain in the Himalayas, in Nepal.

4 Climb the highest mountain in the country.

3 Increase fitness by training. Learn about climbing strategies.

2 Use climbing walls to develop technique.

1 Start going on hiking trips in the hills.

Aber Education

Activity 17	Climbing to Success (2)

Think back to the steps that led up to the summit of Mt Everest.

Have a go at planning the steps you will need to take to achieve one of your long-term goals.

Remember it has to be something that you **really** believe you can achieve. Think about your strengths and weaknesses and use these to clarify your goals.

Your goal doesn't have to be something as dangerous as climbing Mt Everest. It may be that you want to write a novel or you may want to become a newsreader. You may want to work overseas or you may want to be a sporting champion.

All of these goals will need careful thought and planning as to how you are actually going to achieve them.

Now have a quick brainstorm and write down some things you are going to need to develop to achieve your goal.

Write your goal in the space at the top of the mountain.

Now for each stage of the mountain, provide details of an action plan that will allow you to achieve your goal. Think of the points you will need to develop and write them in the space in the mountains.

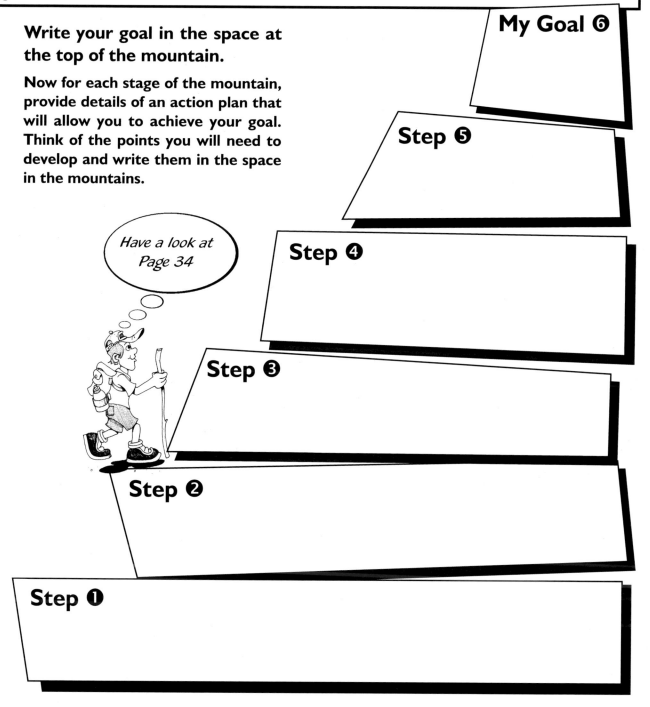

Have a look at Page 34

My Goal ❻

Step ❺

Step ❹

Step ❸

Step ❷

Step ❶

| Activity 18 | If I Could Be Anyone ... |

☞ *The Happiness Fairy has granted you a wish! Your wish is that you can choose to be anyone you like. You have to tell the Happiness Fairy who you would like to be and why, before she will make your wish come true.*

Who you choose depends entirely on you – your "person" may be famous, he/she may be someone you know such as a relative or a friend, or he/she may be an important member of your community. This person can be absolutely anyone on the entire planet.

In your explanation, make sure somewhere that you answer these questions:

❶ Why do I want to be this person?   ❷ What will I be good at?   ❸ Why do I think this person has an interesting life?

| I would like to be ... |

Aber Education

Activity 19	Go On, I Dare You!

☞ *Sometimes people don't do the things they want to achieve because they are scared of failing. They think people will laugh at them or that they don't have the skills or courage to do something.*

Sometimes people don't do the things they want to do because they are scared of things that might happen. People who achieve great things do so because they focus on the task in a POSITIVE way. If someone has a NEGATIVE attitude, then it is unlikely that he/she will be able to achieve their goal.

Look at the comments below. All of these students are about to take part in a cross-country race. Colour in the kids who have a POSITIVE mental attitude.

I am not going to try very hard. There's no point – Sam will win.

I don't think I'll win but you never know!

I am going to run the fastest I have ever run!

I am going to pace myself. I know I can do it.

I won't run. I am no good anyway!

I am no good at cross-country but neither is Chris. We'll run together though.

I've never tried long distance before, but I'll give it a go.

Think About It!

What do you think might have happened if Cathy Freeman had a negative attitude about her 400 metre race at the Sydney Olympics?

Find out who these people are and write about one of their achievements.

❑ Garry Kasparov -

❑ Martina Navratilova -

❑ Bill Gates -

❑ Sir Edmund Hillary -

❑ Mother Teresa -

❑ Sir Weary Dunlop -

Do you think these people had a positive or negative mental attitude about their goals?

Activity 20 About Sport: I'm Positive that I am Not Negative!

☞ *Look at each set of comments below. You will notice that each comment is showing a negative mental attitude about performing in sporting activities. People may have this attitude about themselves, or it may be about other people.*

Have a go at writing POSITIVE statements instead. The first one has been done for you.
As you are completing the activity, colour in the statements that YOU are more likely to say. Do you see yourself as someone who has a negative attitude at times?

Aber Education

Activity 21	About Schoolwork: I'm Positive that I am Not Negative!

☞ *Look at what each of the people is saying below. You will notice that the statements are showing a negative mental attitude about progress with schoolwork. Think about what you might say, you may have even made a negative comment when you first looked at this sheet!*

Have a go at writing POSITIVE statements instead. Next time you hear yourself making a negative statement, stop and ask – "Is this attitude going to help me?" Write positive statements in the empty speech bubbles. The first one has been done for you.

Activity 22 — In a Pickle?

👉 *Everyone has a bad day now and then. This means the happy kid who lives down the street, the captain of the cricket team, the grumpy teenager who works at the supermarket, the lady in the queue at the bank, the prime minister of Britain the nurse that lives next door, the teacher in Room 7 and the KIDS in Room 7. EVERYONE! The trick is to work out how to deal with the bad day.*

When was the last time you felt you were having a bad day? It may even be today! _____

 **Write down some of the things about this day that made you feel bad.**

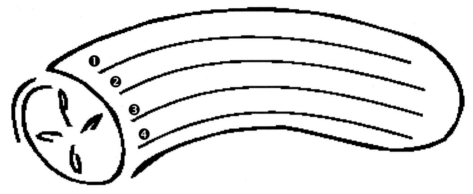

Think about each of the points you have written above. For each point answer the following:

① Was this thing my fault?

② What could have been done to avoid this problem?

③ How did I deal with this problem?

Write your thoughts in the pickles below.

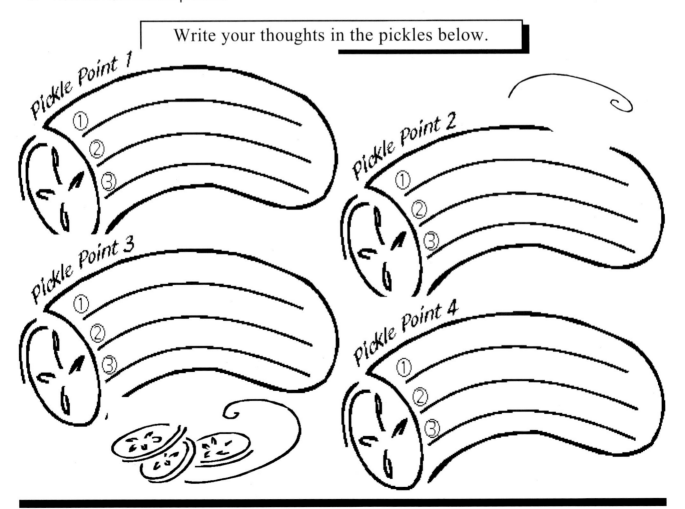

Pickle Point 1

Pickle Point 2

Pickle Point 3

Pickle Point 4

Aber Education

Activity 23 — Helping Myself

☞ *Going for a walk in the fresh air, running along a sandy beach, reading a new book, calling up a friend and listening to your favourite band are some ways that you can turn your day around.*

What are some ways that you have tried to turn a BAD day into a GOOD day?

Write your favourite five:

❶ _____

_____

❷ _____

_____

❸ _____

_____

❹ _____

_____

❺ _____

_____

Brainstorm with a partner and think of some NEW strategies you could use to deal with the pressures of a bad day. They might only be little things, like raking up the leaves in the backyard or sorting out your wardrobe so that it's colour coordinated!

_____

_____

_____

_____

_____

_____

_____

_____

_____

_____

☺ **Cheer Up!**

Now think up four things that you might say to someone who is having a bad day. Think about what you might like to hear when YOU have a bad day.

❶

❷

❸

❹

Activity 24

Talking Heads

Write down a response for each of the boxes below.

Aber Education

Activity 25	A Boring Activity Sheet

 Answer the boring questions below. Be as boring as you like!

❶ Do you ever feel bored?

_____

❷ How do you become bored?

_____

❸ Tick what you do when you're bored.

You can tick more than one.

- ❑ Lie around doing nothing
- ❑ Sleep
- ❑ Complain to everyone that you are bored
- ❑ Sit and wonder why you are bored
- ❑ Ring up friends
- ❑ Cause trouble
- ❑ Get angry with people
- ❑ Eat
- ❑ Go outside
- ❑ Watch boring television
- ❑ Find something to do
- ❑ Other (describe exactly how boring it can all be!)

_____

_____

_____

Boredom Challenges

① **How long can you look at this empty box before becoming bored?**

Write your answer in the box.

② **Where is the most boring place that you have been to?**

_____

③ **What is the most boring book you ever**

_____

read?

_____

④ **What is the most boring show on television?**

_____

⑤ **Who is the most boring singer you have ever heard?**

_____

⑥ **What is the most boring animal in the world?**

_____

⑦ **What is the most boring sport you have ever watched?**

_____

⑧ **What is the most boring method of transport?**

_____

Activity 26	An Even More Boring Sheet!

Make a list of your TOP 10 most boring things you could do!

❶ _____

_____

❷ _____

_____

❸ _____

_____

❹ _____

_____

❺ _____

_____

❻ _____

_____

❼ _____

_____

❽ _____

_____

❾ _____

_____

❿ _____

_____

When were you last feeling bored?

(Obviously you have not been bored while doing this exciting sheet!)

_____

How long did the boredom last for?

_____

Excitement Extravaganza!

Brainstorm to think of all the exciting activities you could do to keep yourself amused. Try to think of things that don't cost any money – things that you could do with friends or your brothers or sisters. This does not include things like watching television or playing computer games.

Group your ideas in a meaningful way and create heading and sub-headings to organise your amazing ideas.

_____

_____

_____

_____

_____

_____

_____

_____

_____

_____

_____

_____

_____

_____

_____

_____

_____

_____

_____

_____

_____

_____

Aber Education

Activity 27 — The Most Boring Day

❶ What would be the most boring day for you ever? Describe it and include EVERY boring detail.

_____

_____

_____

_____

_____

_____

_____

_____

_____

_____

_____

_____

_____

_____

_____

_____

_____

_____

_____

_____

❷ Have you ever had a day just like the one you described? When did this day happen? Give reasons for why such a boring day occurred!

_____

_____

_____

_____

❸ Rate TODAY in terms of how boring it has been.

① ② ③ ④ ⑤ ⑥ ⑦ ⑧ ⑨ ⑩

EXCITING ↑
interesting
dull
mind-numbingly BOORING ↓

❹ Why?

_____

_____

_____

❺ What can you do to improve things?

_____

_____

_____

Activity 28	Rescue Plan

☞ *Never be bored again! It's that simple. All you have to do is make a list of all the things you can do if you ever find yourself at a loose end or with no plans.*

Ask your teacher if you can type up your list on the computer. Print the list out and keep a copy in your tray and one at home. Refer to it WHENEVER YOU ARE BORED!

Activities I can do on my own:

- Make a detailed list of everything that is in my bedroom.

- _____

- _____

- _____

Activities I can do with/for a pet:

- Make a new toy trapeze for the budgie.

- _____

- _____

- _____

Activities I can do in the classroom:

- Create an anti-boredom sign for the wall _____ (think of a funny slogan).

- _____

- _____

- _____

Activities I can do with a friend at home:

- Create a picture book for a little brother or sister.

- _____

- _____

- _____

Activities I can do outdoors:

- Find out the names of the birds in the garden by checking in library books.

- _____

- _____

- _____

Activities I can do during school holidays:

- Make a family photo collage. (You will have to check with your parents about the photos you can use.)

- _____

- _____

- _____

Aber Education

Teachers' Notes: Board Game for the Bored

This activity is designed to extend students' creativity by encouraging them to create a game that small groups of students can play. The idea is that they "borrow" from some of the popular board games currently available to create their own activity.

Materials:

❑ Stiff card - could also use heavy cardboard (from a box) with plain paper stuck to the front. Alternatively, normal card can be used and then covered in Contact® or laminated.

❑ Scissors, glue, coloured paper, coloured markers, dice
Provide all sorts of odds and ends for students to add to their game.

❑ Selection of scrap material (e.g. students could make every fourth square a "felt" square with special instructions.

❑ Magazines (e.g. students could cut out celebrity heads and paste onto the back of cards)

❑ Newspaper (e.g. students could cut out letters from headlines to give their design a "ransom note" look.

Time Frame:

This is not a one-lesson activity. Students will need sufficient time to plan their game and work out how players will proceed to the end.

To encourage creativity, announce that there will be a competition with several categories. The awards will be decided after each student has been able to participate in each game, so this may take some weeks – you may like to run this activity over a term, allowing students to accept feedback about their game and giving them time to make modifications and revisions.

When planning the awards ceremony, remember that the more awards offered the better, as ideally it would enhance individual students' Self-Esteem if each student were able to receive an award.

Awards for certain categories could be decided by a vote from all students. You may even like to have a "Reality-TV" style voting competition

running through the term. Add more categories depending on student's work.

Some ideas for award categories include:

❑ Best board design

❑ The hardest game

❑ Best use of colour

❑ Best use of drawings

❑ Best use of words

❑ Best use of images

❑ Most creative game

❑ Best use of funny sayings

❑ Most crazy game

❑ Most unusual game

❑ Most clever game

❑ Funniest game

❑ Most annoying game

❑ Most non-boring game

❑ Game with the most variety

❑ Most original game

❑ Longest game

❑ Most strangest game

❑ The People's Choice Award

❑ The game you would most like to be stuck on a desert island with.

❑ Most brain-taxing game

Activity 29	Board Game for the Bored

CHALLENGE!

☞ *You are the chairperson of THE BORED. You must devise a board game that will stop you and your friends from being bored.*

Plan your "bored" game below and remember you will need to provide clear instructions. You want your board game to be popular with the other students so try extra hard to make it a fun and original game. Here are some ideas to get you started.

To get from the start to the finish, students might have to:

• use activities like drawing (e.g. Pictionary), • participate in miming activities (e.g. Charades),
• answer questions (e.g. Trivial Pursuit), • perform or tell a joke, • use a combination of all of the above.

Plan your board game design below. Your teacher will tell you about the materials you can use.

Now create the final game. Use some large sheets of stiff card to make the board and any cards that are needed. Be as crazy as you want with the design, it doesn't have to be a square shape – squares are boring!

Then ask your teacher for some features to add to your game, such as newspapers, magazines, scrap materials. If you're not that flash at drawing you can use all sorts of other ways to make your board game eye-catching. (e.g. Print things out from the computer.)

Remember there are awards in several categories for the best game! Everyone in the class will have a turn at playing your game.

Aber Education